BIRDS OF NORTH

Writer
Stan Freeman

Illustrators
Mike Nasuti
and Rob Chapin

Photo Editor
Domingo "Dino"
Diaz, Jr.

Special Consultant
Wayne R. Petersen,
Field Ornithologist,
Massachusetts
Audubon Society

Red-tailed hawk

1

Snowy egret

Science and Nature in Motion
Birds of North America

Published by: Hampshire House Publishing Co.
8 Nonotuck St.
Florence, Mass. 01060

First Printing
Printed on recycled paper in the
United States of America
Copyright © 1996 by Stan Freeman
Illustrations copyright © 1996 by Mike Nasuti and
Rob Chapin

ISBN: 0-9636814-2-7
Library of Congress Catalogue Card Number: 96-75349

The authors would like to thank Barry Schatz, Karin
Henry and Austin Kenefick for their assistance in
editing the manuscript.

Front cover: Bald eagles; back cover: Atlantic puffins

Gray catbirds

CONTENTS

BIRDS IN MOTION

To see a great egret landing, a bald eagle fishing, a brown pelican taking off and tundra swans flying, flip the page edges.

Northern saw-whet owl

Ring-billed gull

CONTENTS

American kestrel

Blue jay

BIRDS OF
NORTH AMERICA

Here are profiles of 74 of the more common birds seen in the United States and Canada, with photographs as well as maps of each bird's winter, year-round and breeding ranges.

INTRODUCTION

Great egret landing

Brown pelican taking off

Almost any place you go on earth you will be able to see a bird flying overhead sooner or later, whether it's in the middle of the ocean or on top of the highest mountain. One reason is that there may be 100 billion birds in the world, nearly 20 birds for every person.

From golden eagles and purple finches to white-throated sparrows and ring-necked ducks, there may be more than 9,000 different kinds or species of birds in the world and more than 800 species that have been seen in North America.

Canada geese

How did birds get their remarkable features, their wings and feathers, as well as their beautiful songs and rainbow of colors? The earliest birds probably did not look much like birds today. They may have looked more like lizards. The first true bird may have been the Archaeopteryx, which lived 140 million years ago. It had feathered wings and probably glided for short distances as it hunted.

Archaeopteryx

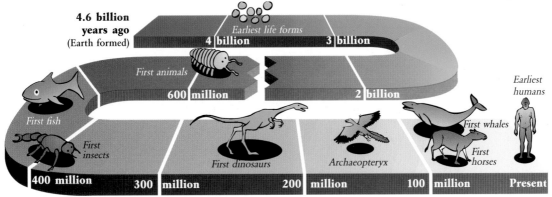

4.6 billion years ago
(Earth formed)

Earliest life forms

4 billion

3 billion

First animals

600 million

2 billion

First fish

First insects

First dinosaurs

Archaeopteryx

First whales

First horses

Earliest humans

400 million

300 million

200 million

100 million

Present

Over time, the features of birds changed through the process of evolution. When a bird was born with a feature that gave it a slight advantage over other birds, such as a sharper beak that was better for hunting, it had a better chance for survival because it could get food more easily than birds with beaks that were not as sharp.

Great egret landing

Brown pelican taking off

Peregrine falcon

And when it became a parent, some of its chicks might inherit its sharper beak and they too would have a better chance for survival. Soon the birds with sharper beaks would become more plentiful than birds with beaks that were not as sharp.

Other features of birds, such as size, coloring and eyesight, evolved in the same way over many years.

The long neck and cupped beak of a flamingo evolved to help it sift through water for small fish and other food. Its long legs help it wade through water.

Golden-fronted woodpecker

The strong, pointed beak of a woodpecker evolved so it could peck holes in trees to hollow out its nest and to find insects under the bark. Its grasping claws and long, stiff tail hold it in place on the side of a tree as it pecks at the wood.

The small size and strong wing muscles of a hummingbird evolved so that it could hover at flowers like a bee. Its long bill allows it to drink the rich nectar deep inside flowers.

Flamingo

Ruby-throated hummingbird (female)

Birds come in all sizes, from hummingbirds, which may be shorter than your thumb and weigh less than a penny, to ostriches, which can grow to be more than 8 feet tall and weigh more than 300 pounds.

Great egret landing

Brown pelican taking off

Ostrich, 8 feet

Great blue heron, 4 feet

Bald eagle, 2.5 feet

American crow, 1 foot

House sparrow, 4 inches

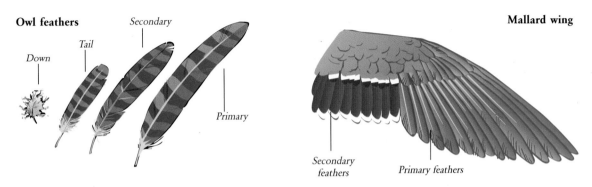

Owl feathers

Down

Tail

Secondary

Primary

Mallard wing

Secondary feathers

Primary feathers

Feathers are a bird's clothing, keeping it warm in winter, cool in summer and dry in the rain. A robin might have 3,000 feathers on its body, and a tundra swan might have as many as 25,000. Beneath a bird's outer feathers are soft, puffy down feathers that provide extra warmth.

Once a feather grows to full size, it slowly begins to die.

Peacock

Most birds have to replace most of their feathers once or twice a year through a process called molting. Molting requires so much energy that once the process begins, many birds will stop singing, stop fighting and keep to themselves during the time it takes the new feathers to grow, which is sometimes a month or more.

Great egret landing

Brown pelican taking off

Most of the visible feathers on a bird have a hard central shaft and smaller shafts growing from each side of the central shaft. The smaller shafts stay together because of tiny barbs or hooks growing between them. These barbs act like tiny zippers.

When the barbs are all zipped up, the feather is resistant to air and water. But if the barbs become unhooked in flight, a bird will stop to preen itself by running the feather through its bill to zip up the barbs again.

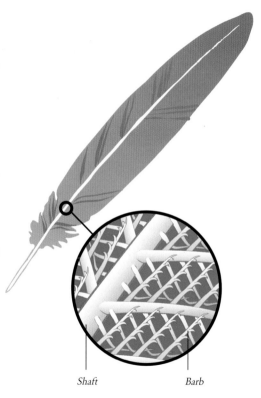

Shaft   Barb

COLORING

Birds can have brilliant coloring, but its purpose is not to please the human eye. In most land birds, the male has the more distinctive feather colors to better attract females. For instance, a male northern cardinal is bright red over most of its feathers, while the female is buff-olive and dull red.

During the breeding season, some male birds may look almost nothing like the females of their species.

Because bright colors might also attract predators, which are birds and other animals that might hunt them for food, many male birds grow their brightest feathers in the spring, when they are trying to attract mates. But they often change them when they molt later in the summer and then have plainer coloring through the winter.

Male house finch (right) with female

Male evening grosbeak (right) with female

Female mallard

Male mallard

Male cardinal (right) feeding female

Great egret landing

Brown pelican taking off

The coloring of birds also helps disguise them for protection against predators. In bright sunny areas, many birds have evolved to have yellowish-green coloring to blend with their surroundings. Birds that spend much of their time in bushes are often brown. Coloring also helps to disguise birds as they search for food, helping them sneak up on insects and small animals without being noticed as quickly.

Purple gallinule

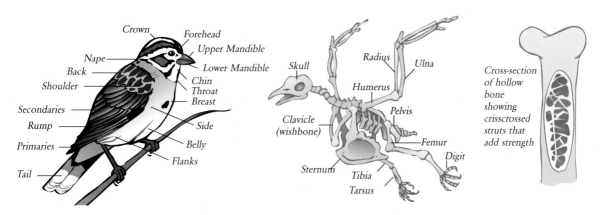

Crown
Forehead
Upper Mandible
Nape
Lower Mandible
Back
Chin
Shoulder
Throat
Secondaries
Breast
Rump
Side
Primaries
Belly
Flanks
Tail

Skull
Radius
Ulna
Humerus
Clavicle (wishbone)
Pelvis
Femur
Digit
Sternum
Tibia
Tarsus

Cross-section of hollow bone showing crisscrossed struts that add strength

To fly, birds must be as light as possible, so many of their bones have evolved to be hollow and filled with air. Flying also requires a great deal of energy, so birds have developed large hearts that can beat very rapidly. A human heart beats about 72 times a minute, but an excited canary's heart may beat 1,000 times a minute.

Most birds also breathe faster than human beings. Small birds, even when resting, breathe 100 to 200 times a minute compared with a rate of 10 to 20 times a minute for human beings.

Although the senses of taste and smell are generally thought to be poor in most birds, their hearing can be very sharp, and their vision is the keenest in the animal kingdom. It is believed hawks can see up to eight times as much detail as humans because they have eight times as many vision cells in their eyes.

With their heads held still, people can see only in front of them because their eyes are positioned toward the front of their heads. But some birds, like woodcocks, have their eyes more on the sides of their heads and are able to see in a complete circle around them.

Birds also have an extra eyelid through which they can partially see. When they are underwater or flying into the wind, they close it and it protects their eyes like a pair of goggles.

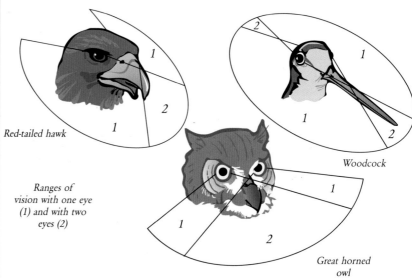

Red-tailed hawk

Woodcock

Ranges of vision with one eye (1) and with two eyes (2)

Great horned owl

Birds have a special curved shape to their wings that helps them fly. Airplane wings have a similar shape.

Ring-billed gulls

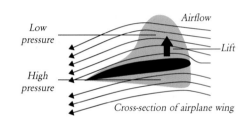

Cross-section of airplane wing

In flight, air flows past the top of a bird's wing faster than it flows past the bottom because of this special curved shape. This faster moving air does not press down on the wing as hard as the slower moving air below the wing is pressing up. This difference in air pressure – a larger pressure pushing up than down – helps a bird stay in the air. It creates "lift" on the wing.

Great egret landing

Brown pelican taking off

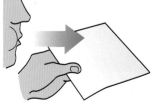

Carolina chickadee

To see how lift is created, take a piece of paper and hold it as in the illustration above. Blow just across the top of the paper. The loose end of the paper should rise slightly. That's because the fast-moving air above the paper creates an area of air pressure that is lower above the paper than it is below.

If you have ever held your flattened hand just a few inches out the window of a moving car, you probably noticed that when you tilted your hand at different angles, your hand was forced up or down depending on the angle. Birds take advantage of this when they fly, tilting their wings to climb higher or to dive lower.

Ross' gull

If the wing is tilted up slightly, like this...

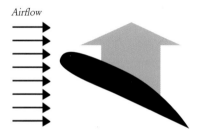

Airflow

...the lift increases because the air strikes the bottom side of the wing at more of an angle, pushing up on it even harder, creating climbing flight.

Tilting the wing down causes the rushing air to push down on the wing, creating diving flight.

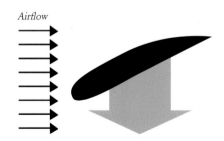

Airflow

Great egret landing

Brown pelican taking off

Birds can fly by flapping their wings, but they can also glide, soar and hover.

In flapping flight, it is mainly the downstroke of the wings that keeps a bird up in the air and moves it forward. During the downstroke, the wings are stretched out and the wing feathers are linked together, creating the most possible resistance to the air and therefore the greatest push against the air.

During the upstroke, a bird bends its wings so that it can move them back up through the air with the least possible resistance. Many birds also spread apart their wing feathers during the upstroke so that the air flows between the feathers, also lowering the air resistance.

Downstroke of a great blue heron

Upstroke of a mallard

By spreading their wings and holding them still, most birds can glide on air, sometimes for great distances. For instance, a pigeon drops about one foot for every ten feet that it glides forward.

When steam escapes from a pot of boiling water on a stove, it rises to the ceiling. Hot air on the land also rises, and birds can take free rides up into the sky on these streams of hot air, which are called thermals. This type of flying is called soaring. Birds simply glide and let the hot-air current carry them higher like a kite on the wind.

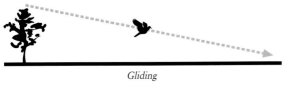

Gliding

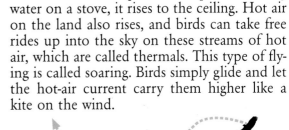

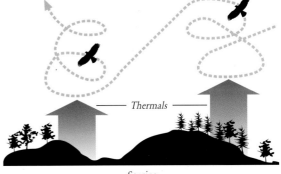

Thermals

Soaring

Hummingbirds and rough-legged hawks can hover in midair, staying in one place by rapidly flapping their wings.

Hovering

The larger the bird, generally the faster it can fly, although there are some small birds that can be very swift fliers.

Finches and sparrows can reach flying speeds of 20 miles per hour, hawks can fly up to 40 miles per hour, and ducks and geese can fly 60 miles per hour. The fastest flying speeds are reached by streamlined birds, such as peregrine falcons, when they go into a dive, perhaps 120 to 200 miles per hour.

Great egret landing

Brown pelican taking off

American kestrel

WINGS

The pointed wings of a barn swallow let it dart and turn at high speeds in flight.

The long, narrow wings of a wandering albatross help it glide for great distances over the ocean.

The long, broad wings of a red-tailed hawk let it soar for great distances over the land.

Tundra swans flying

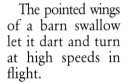

Bald eagle fishing

In general, the smaller the bird, the faster it beats its wings in flight. A crow might beat its wings three to five times a second, and a yellow warbler might have as many as 14 wing beats a second.

Some hummingbirds, when they are hovering, might beat their tiny wings an astounding 70 times each second, so quickly that the wings appear only as a blur to the human eye.

Great egret landing

Brown pelican taking off

The short, thick beak of a finch helps it crack open seeds.

The hooked beak of an eagle is used for killing and tearing apart the prey it captures for food.

The long, thin beak of an American avocet is used to grab small fish and insects out of shallow water.

The curved claws of a chickadee help it to hold on securely to branches when it perches.

The sharp claws or talons of an osprey are used to capture fish for food.

The broad, flat tail of the northern cardinal acts as a rudder in flight and a brake when landing.

Tundra swans flying

Bald eagle fishing

Great egret landing

Brown pelican taking off

Songs are the language of birds. Birds sing to tell other birds a certain territory is theirs or to attract a mate. Some people believe they also sing to use up excess energy.

The small birds you might see perching on a branch or fence, such as robins or sparrows, are called songbirds. Their songs, and the songs of other birds that sing, usually are made up of a series of sounds and musical notes repeated over and over again.

What the songs and calls of different birds may sound like:

Rufous-sided towhee – "Drink your tea!"

Acadian flycatcher – "Pizza!"

Gray catbird – "Meow!"

Ovenbird – "Teacher, teacher, teacher!"

Yellow-headed blackbird

For instance, the song of a robin sounds like "Cheerily, cheer-up!" When a robin sings, it repeats its song over and over again. The loud, ringing song of the Carolina wren sounds like "Tea-kettle, tea-kettle, tea-kettle!"

In one day, a bobwhite was heard to sing its song 1,400 times, and a sparrow sang its song 2,300 times. One red-eyed vireo was heard to sing its short song, which lasts only a second, 22,000 times in just 10 hours!

Tundra swans flying

Double-crested cormorant (immature)

Bell's vireo – "Tweedle-deedle-dum? Tweedle-deedle-dee!"

Tufted titmouse – "Peter, Peter, Peter!"

Laughing gull – "Hah, hah, hah!"

Olive-sided flycatcher – "Quick three beers!"

Bald eagle fishing

Great egret landing

Brown pelican taking off

Males are usually the more impressive singers, although in some species, such as the cardinal, the female's song may be almost as beautiful as the male's.

Most species have two or more distinct songs, as well as a variety of other calls and notes, that send other birds certain messages. For instance, one call may warn of danger while another may say the danger is past.

The songs of each species do not usually change very much from place to place. The song of a blue jay will sound pretty much the same anywhere in the world blue jays can be found.

Northern bobwhite – "Poor Bob White!"

Common poorwill – "Poor Will!"

White-throated sparrow – "Poor Sam Peabody, Peabody, Peabody!"

Great horned owl – "Who, who-who-who, who, who!"

Indigo bunting

Since spring is the time of year when birds usually search for mates and claim a territory for nesting, that is the season when songs are most frequently heard.

Most birds sing during the day. A robin might start at dawn, slow down during the heat of the afternoon, and pick up again before sunset and then stop. The wood thrush is at its best around sunset. But whip-poor-wills and owls might sing or call through the night.

Tundra swans flying

Red-winged blackbird

Steller's jay – "Shack, shack, shack, shack!"

Red-winged blackbird – "Ok-a-lee!"

Wood thrush – "Ee-oh-lay!"

Common yellowthroat – "Witchity, witchity, witchity, witch!"

Bald eagle fishing

29

Birds like to sing while perched on a tree branch or in a bush. But a few, like the goldfinch, often sing while flying.

The woodpecker, which has a poor singing voice, will use its bill to drum on a drain pipe, metal roof or other object, trying to make the loudest noise possible instead of singing a song.

White-breasted nuthatch – "Yank, yank!"

White-eyed vireo – "Quick give me the rain check!"

Blue jay – "Thief, thief!"

Chestnut-sided warbler – "Pleased, pleased, pleased to meet you!"

Great egret landing

Brown pelican taking off

Grasshopper sparrow

Among birds, it is usually the male's job to attract the female during courtship. A male will stake out a territory, claiming it as his own. Then he may sing or put on flying displays or show his colorful tail or wing feathers to convince a female to choose him as a mate.

Most birds select a new mate each breeding season, but some, like swans and eagles, will choose one mate for life.

Tundra swans flying

Male greater prarie-chicken "booming" to attract a female

Bald eagle fishing

Great egret landing

Brown pelican taking off

Just as most people want to own a home with a yard around it, most birds also like to claim an area of land as their own territory where they can build their nests and hunt for food.

The larger the bird, usually the larger the territory. Eagles might claim a square mile as theirs, fiercely defending it against other eagles who might wander into it. However, robins may settle for territories that are as small as 70 feet wide and 70 feet long.

Typical American robin territories

Different species of birds can peacefully share the same territory. A male hawk will mainly guard against other male hawks who might want to steal away his mate or his territory.

It is usually the job of the male to find a suitable territory for nesting and then to attract a female to join him there. Once a nest is built, it is also usually the job of the male to patrol and defend the territory against intruders while the female cares for the young.

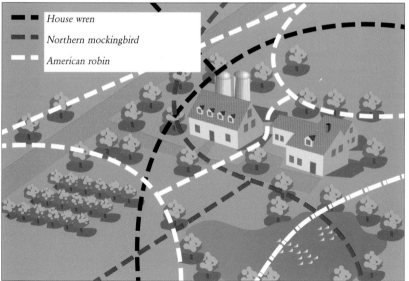

Territory sharing

Tundra swans flying

Bald eagle fishing

33

Different birds build different kinds of nests in which to lay their eggs. One of the most common types is a cup-shaped nest built of twigs or grass in the fork formed by two tree branches.

Almost anything in nature is used in building nests. Terns use seashells, doves use sticks, killdeer use pebbles, and hummingbirds use spider webs and plant fibers.

Great egret landing

Brown pelican taking off

Red-eyed vireo nest

A nest can be built at the very top of a tree, like that of the eagle, or in a hole in the ground, like the nest of the kingfisher. A woodpecker pecks a hole in a tree for its nest. Sea birds often build nests on rocky ledges of ocean cliffs, and chimney swifts build their nests in chimneys.

The largest nests are those of eagles and ospreys. They can be 8 feet across and 15 feet deep and weigh 4,000 pounds, which is heavier than some automobiles!

Ospreys at their nest

Tundra swans flying

Bald eagle fishing

Great egret landing

Brown pelican taking off

Most songbirds lay three to six eggs to fill their nests, but some quails and pheasants lay as many as 20 eggs.

The female usually sits on the eggs to keep them warm until they hatch. Eggs of songbirds may take 10 to 20 days to hatch. The eggs of an albatross may take up to 79 days. A baby bird finally breaks out of its egg by pecking a hole in the shell.

Loon egg

Black-bellied plover eggs

Canada
goose

*Eggs vary in size
from the largest,
those of the
ostrich, which are
more than 6 inches
long, to the
smallest, those of
the hummingbird,
which can be
about the size of a
pea. The eggs
shown here are
actual size.*

American
crow

Ruby-throated
hummingbird

American
robin

Great
horned
owl

Tundra swans flying

Bald eagle fishing

Many birds, including songbirds, are born blind and helpless. They come out of their shells without any feathers and are unable to open their eyes for several days. They may not leave the nest and their parent's warmth and protection for two weeks or more.

Barn swallow nestlings

Even after songbirds venture from the nest for their first flight, they may still need the protection of their parents for another two or three weeks.

Other birds, such as ducks, grouse and killdeer, are more developed at hatching. They will have a thick layer of down feathers that keeps them warm on their own. Some, such as killdeer, have strong enough legs to leave the nest within hours of hatching.

By the time most young birds leave the nest, they will reach close to their full body size and have all their feathers.

A peregrine falcon hatchling being fed

Tundra swans flying

Bald eagle fishing

Bald eagles and other larger birds may spend up to three months in the nest before they can fly away. A bird's first attempt to fly can sometimes be awkward. While still in the nest, young birds will test their wings by flapping them as if they were actually flying. The first flight may be very short, possibly from the nest to a near-by branch or ledge. But usually within days, a young bird will have mastered most of the skills needed to be a successful flier.

Young red-shouldered hawks nearly ready to leave the nest

FOOD

Birds are often specialists when it comes to eating. They generally prefer one kind of food over all others. Canada geese like grass, ospreys eat fish, warblers look for insects, and finches like seeds. However, most birds will eat more than one type of food, and some birds change their diets with the seasons.

Because they burn so much energy while flying, birds can have very large appetites. Many songbirds will eat nearly half their weight in food each day, especially during migration.

House wren

What different birds like to eat:

Bald eagle – fish, waterfowl, dead animals.

Great horned owl – mice, snakes, rabbits, opossums, frogs, skunks, small birds.

American robin – earthworms, insects, fruit, berries.

Northern mockingbird – insects, fruit, berries.

Common tern – fish.

Great egret – fish, frogs, crayfish, insects.

Red-headed woodpecker – insects, acorns, berries, fruit.

Broad-tailed hummingbird – flower nectar, small insects.

Tundra swans flying

Bald eagle fishing

Over millions of years, birds have learned to migrate in the fall from areas where food is becoming more scarce and the weather is turning too cold to survive to areas with warmer climates and an abundance of food.

In the United States and Canada in September and October, great flocks of birds sometimes fill the sky as they fly south, often to South and Central America, to spend the winter. Nearly two-thirds of the birds in North America migrate.

Great egret landing

Brown pelican taking off

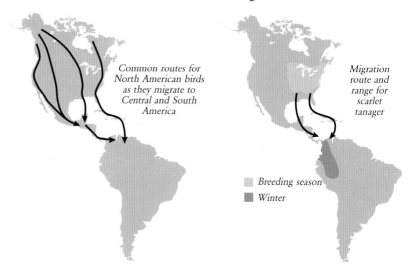

Common routes for North American birds as they migrate to Central and South America

Migration route and range for scarlet tanager

Breeding season
Winter

Some birds migrate together in huge flocks filled with many different kinds of birds. But some, like Canada geese and chimney swifts, travel only with their own species. Falcons and owls travel alone.

The height at which birds fly during migration varies greatly. Many seabirds travel just a few feet above the water. But some larger birds, such as geese, may fly several miles high, sometimes rising above the clouds so that they can fly in clear skies.

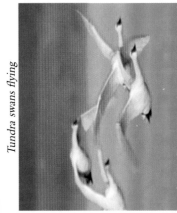

Tundra swans flying

Bald eagle fishing

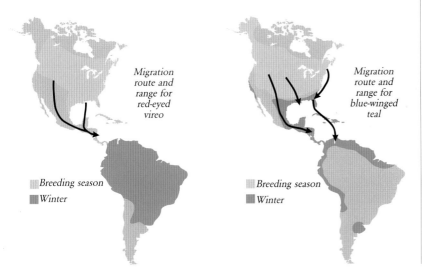

Migration route and range for red-eyed vireo

Breeding season
Winter

Migration route and range for blue-winged teal

Breeding season
Winter

Great egret landing

Brown pelican taking off

Bad weather and strong winds often affect the migration habits of birds. They may fly either higher or lower to escape heavy clouds, and some will seek out winds at certain heights that may help them fly faster.

Many birds can travel 200 to 300 miles a day during the migration. Some, like ducks and hawks, travel during the daytime, but most smaller birds travel at night. They stop to rest and eat during the day.

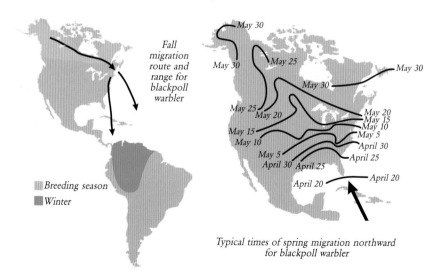

Fall migration route and range for blackpoll warbler

Breeding season
Winter

May 30
May 30   May 25
May 30
May 30
May 20
May 25
May 20
May 15
May 15
May 10
May 10
May 5
April 30
May 5
April 30   April 25
April 20
April 20
April 25

Typical times of spring migration northward for blackpoll warbler

Scientists believe the shorter days, changes in nighttime star patterns and colder temperatures of autumn are among the things that might trigger the urge in birds to migrate. They believe the stars or magnetic north pole may help guide birds during the migration, as might landmarks like mountains and coastlines. But it is still something of a mystery how birds can fly thousands of miles, often over the ocean, to exactly the same winter home, sometimes even to the same tree, and then return north each spring to the same nesting grounds.

Tundra swans flying

Snow geese

Bald eagle fishing

Great egret landing

Brown pelican taking off

You will rarely see a sleeping bird. Most choose out-of-the-way places to sleep, such as tree cavities or thick brush, for protection from predators. Some birds sleep while perched on branches. When they squat down, tendons in their feet automatically tighten, closing their toes around the branch so that they are held securely in place. Some birds, such as crows and starlings, sleep in large flocks, called roosts, for mutual protection and for added warmth.

Starlings forming their roost at dusk

LIFE SPAN

Some larger birds, such as eagles and pelicans, can live almost as long as people, 50 or even 60 years, when they live in zoos or other protected places. But in the wild, where birds can fall victim to diseases, accidents, a lack of food, harsh weather and hunting by people as well as by other animals, their lives are usually shorter.

The maximum life span of eagles in the wild may be 30 to 35 years. Hawks, swans and ducks can live 20 to 25 years. But most small songbirds may live only two to five years.

Atlantic puffin

Tundra swans flying

Bald eagle fishing

Maximum recorded life span in years for some birds in the wild:

Arctic tern – 34	Great horned owl – 17	Sanderling – 12
Great blue heron – 23	Northern cardinal – 15	Song sparrow – 11
Mallard – 23	American robin – 13	Dark-eyed junco – 10
Atlantic puffin – 21	House sparrow – 13	Scarlet tanager – 10
Brown pelican – 19	Wild turkey - 12	House wren – 7

Great egret landing

Brown pelican taking off

No one will ever again see a passenger pigeon or a Carolina parakeet in flight. They are birds that no longer exist, that are extinct, because they were hunted by people until none were left alive.

Many species of birds have faced, and still do face, threats to their survival from hunting or destruction of the places in which they nest. But today, most birds are protected from hunting by laws, and in some places where the rarest birds live and nest, the building of houses, businesses and roads is not allowed.

Carolina parakeet

Passenger pigeon

BIRD FEEDERS

A bird feeder will bring birds right into your back yard, even to your window, so you can watch them more closely throughout the year. Feeders can be hung from tree branches or be placed atop poles in the ground. They can be filled with seed or grains or a mixture of other foods to attract a variety of birds. Sunflower seeds are liked by most birds that visit feeders.

Tundra swans flying

Bald eagle fishing

Great egret landing

Brown pelican taking off

Birds are the wildlife you are most likely to see where you live, whether it is in a large city or a small town. On the following pages, you will find information about 74 of the most common birds seen in North America.

Many birds migrate to warmer regions when winter approaches. Maps are provided for each bird to show the limits of where it can be found in North America during its breeding season (usually spring and summer), during the winter and year-round. However, the limits are always changing as birds widen or narrow their ranges, so the maps should be used only as general guides.

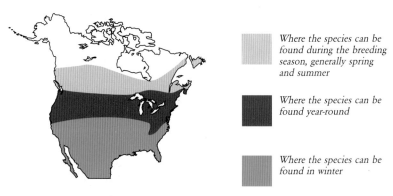

Where the species can be found during the breeding season, generally spring and summer

Where the species can be found year-round

Where the species can be found in winter

If a bird's breeding range is shown on the map but its winter range is not shown, it means the bird spends its winters in Central or South America.

Length

Tundra swans flying

Also provided is the average length of each species of bird as measured from the tip of its bill to the end of its tail. However, individual birds can be quite a bit longer or shorter than the species average.

Bald eagle fishing

On pages 110 and 111, you will find photographs of common backyard birds, a guide to help you more quickly identify those birds you may see near where you live.

Great egret landing

Brown pelican taking off

10"

American robins are probably the most familiar songbirds in North America. Robins can often be seen standing on lawns, their heads cocked to one side, as if listening for something. Actually, they are searching the ground for one of their favorite foods, earthworms. Robins usually build cup-shaped nests in trees or shrubs, but sometimes they will construct a nest right on the windowsill of a house. They may use grass and weed stalks that are held together with dried mud. The female carries the mud to the nest in her bill, pressing it into place with her body.

Bullock's Oriole

8"

These bright, orange and black birds can be seen in open woodlands and in shade trees around homes. They use plant fibers and bits of bark to build nests that look like baskets and hang from the tips of branches high up in trees. The oriole in the West is called the Bullock's oriole. The eastern species is called the Baltimore oriole.

Baltimore Oriole

8"

Tundra swans flying

Bald eagle fishing

53

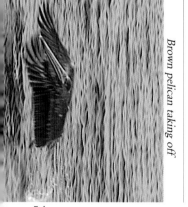

Great egret landing

Brown pelican taking off

8½"

With their red shoulder patches, male redwings are often seen perched atop cattails in a marsh or swamp, overseeing their territories, which they will energetically defend. They will even attack larger birds, such as hawks and crows, that come near. Redwings usually nest in brush-filled wetland areas. The male often courts the female by chasing her about and flashing his red shoulder markings. In the fall and winter, red-winged blackbirds may be seen mixed into great flocks of blackbirds that search for leftover seeds in farm fields. Female redwings are brown with heavy streaks.

Northern Cardinal

8½"

Cardinals are beautiful birds that are also excellent singers. Their song may sound like "What cheer! What cheer! Wit! Wit! Wit!" They are often seen in city parks and back yards. Once a cardinal chooses its mate for the season, wherever you see the buff-colored female, you will usually see the bright red male nearby. They build their nests in dense shrubbery, thickets or small trees. They may raise three or even four broods of young a year.

Tundra swans flying

Bald eagle fishing

Great egret landing

Brown pelican taking off

Tanagers are among the most beautiful North American birds, but they can be difficult to spot in the wild. They prefer dense forests. Scarlet tanagers often sit motionless in the tops of trees for long periods. Tanagers have loud songs, which may sound like a poor version of a robin's song.

Scarlet Tanager

7"

Eastern Meadowlark

9"

These two species can be hard to tell apart. Their songs help to identify them. The eastern meadowlark's song may sound like a whistled "Spring of the year!" The song of the western meadowlark sounds like a series of loud, flute-like whistles. Meadowlarks often sing while perched on fences or telephone lines. As their name suggests, they prefer meadows, pastures and prairies.

Western Meadowlark

9"

Tundra swans flying

Bald eagle fishing

57

Great egret landing

Brown pelican taking off

Summer coloring

5"

Finches like to travel in flocks and are frequent visitors to feeders, especially if thistle seeds are on the menu. Goldfinches are some-

times called "wild canaries" because of the male's rich yellow color in summer. In winter, the male's plumage turns a greenish yellow, which is closer to the color the female has year-round. Goldfinches have a flight call that sounds like "Per-chick-o-ree!"

Winter coloring

House Finch

5½"

House finches and purple finches are often mistaken for each other. Purple finches are stockier than house finches, and the coloring of the male purple finch is a deeper red, a shade that is closer to raspberry. In the East, house finches can be found in residential areas. In the West, they are more often found in open fields, brushy deserts and orchards.

Purple Finch

6"

Tundra swans flying

Bald eagle fishing

Great egret landing

Brown pelican taking off

Evening Grosbeak

8"

Grosbeaks, as their name implies, have large, strong bills that are ideal for cracking open seeds. Evening grosbeaks often travel in large flocks that suddenly alight in an area to feed on tree buds and seeds. These birds have gradually moved their range east, perhaps because of the increasing number of feeders stocked with sunflower seeds. However, in the East, they are mainly seen in winter.

Rose-breasted Grosbeak

8"

The rose-breasted grosbeak is to the East what the black-headed grosbeak is to the West. Their songs are similar, sounding much like a robin's song. Also, the male of both species will help incubate the eggs, sitting on them while the female forages for food. Females of both species are largely brown with streaking and yellow wing linings.

Black-headed Grosbeak

7"

Tundra swans flying

Bald eagle fishing

Great egret landing

Brown pelican taking off

Yellow Warbler

5"

These bright-yellow birds like to be near water and are usually spotted close to swamps, marshes or river bottoms. Their song may sound like "Sweet, sweet, oh, so sweet!" Yellow warblers spend little time in their breeding territory. They may arrive in late April, build nests, raise their young, and be on their way back to their winter territories in the tropics by the end of July. Yellow warblers usually build their nests in the forks of tree branches, weaving together milkweed fibers, fine grasses, down-like bits of plants and even spider silk to construct a strong, compact cup. They do not visit backyard feeders.

Cedar Waxwing

7"

Tundra swans flying

Bald eagle fishing

If you see one cedar waxwing, the chances are you will see many. Through much of the year, they travel in flocks. They prefer to eat fruits and berries, so they are often spotted in orchards and gardens. Sometimes a line of cedar waxwings will be seen perched on a branch passing berries down from one to the next. Sleek and elegant, cedar waxwings have colors and markings that may almost look as if they were painted on to their feathers.

Great egret landing

Brown pelican taking off

Eastern Bluebird

6½"

Hearing a bluebird's rich song is a sign for many people that spring has arrived. But bluebirds are not as plentiful in many areas as they once were because the nesting sites they prefer - tree cavities such as old woodpecker holes - are no longer as plentiful. Also, these nest sites are sought by an increasing number of other birds. Bluebirds mainly eat insects, such as grasshoppers and beetles, and often they will catch these insects in midair. In winter, they will also eat berries.

Western Bluebird

6½"

Blue Jay

12"

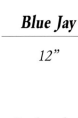

Both of these jays are bold birds with crests and loud piercing calls. Blue jays have striking colors, but their aggressive behavior doesn't please everyone. They are often seen at feeders, pushing aside other birds who get in their way. Steller's jays don't appear at backyard feeders as frequently, but they will visit camp and picnic sites in summer.

Steller's Jay

13"

Tundra swans flying

Bald eagle fishing

Great egret landing

Brown pelican taking off

Tree Swallow

6"

Tree and barn swallows are strong fliers, able to perform impressive maneuvers in midair as they try to capture flying insects, one of their favorite foods. Barn swallows are able to fly as much as 600 miles a day. Tree swallows like to nest in old woodpecker holes and birdhouses. Barn swallows, which have forked tails, make nests of mud and straw that are plastered in barns, sheds and other structures.

Barn Swallow

6½"

Black-capped Chickadee

5½"

Bold, curious, acrobatic birds, chickadees can appear like small fluffy balls of feathers. The black-capped and Carolina chickadees are almost identical in appearance, but their songs, which for both is "Chick-a-dee-dee-dee!" have different deliveries. It is slower and lower when the black-capped chickadee issues it. The black-capped chickadee is more likely to visit a feeder than a Carolina chickadee.

Carolina Chickadee

4½"

Tundra swans flying

Bald eagle fishing

Great egret landing

Brown pelican taking off

6"

Often seen in winter in small flocks, scouring the ground for fallen seeds beneath a feeder, dark-eyed juncos may have different coloring, depending on the region in which they are seen. The "Oregon" race of this species has a black hood and a lighter brown back and flanks, while the "slate-colored" race is nearly black in these areas. Juncos usually build their nests on the ground, sheltered by high grass, logs or fallen trees. The female constructs the nest out of grass, roots, twigs and shreds of bark, and then lines it with fine grass. She usually lays four or five eggs. Juncos may have two broods of young each breeding season.

White-breasted Nuthatch

6"

These small energetic birds have a curious habit. They like to travel headfirst down tree trunks, searching for insects in crevices in the bark. Few other birds search for food in this manner. Both species will visit feeders for sunflower seeds and suet. These nuthatches like to build their nests in hollowed out cavities, such as old woodpecker holes.

Red-breasted Nuthatch

4½"

Tundra swans flying

Bald eagle fishing

Great egret landing

Brown pelican taking off

In the East, the tufted titmouse is a frequent visitor to feeders, darting in and out to grab a seed. The plain titmouse is a shyer bird but will also visit feeders near woodlands. Both these crested birds will hang upside-down from branches as they search for insects on the bark and leaves, and both nest in cavities in trees.

Plain Titmouse

5"

Northern Mockingbird

11"

Tundra swans flying

Bald eagle fishing

Mockingbirds are great mimics, able to imitate the songs of dozens of other birds. They can also imitate barking dogs, musical instruments and police sirens. Mockingbirds are gradually spreading their range northward and can be found in the largest cities and smallest towns. They can often be seen perched high on rooftops, singing loudly and tirelessly. Mockingbirds also sing at night. They are very territorial birds and will even fly at people who venture too close to their nests. They build their nests with twigs, leaves and plant stems 3 to 10 feet off the ground in a tree, shrub or tangle of vines. Mockingbirds usually lay three to five eggs to fill their nest, and they may have two broods of young each breeding season.

Great egret landing

Brown pelican taking off

6"

Sparrows are small birds that often travel in flocks that may be made up of many different species. Brown or gray with streaks, sparrows are usually seed-eaters that feed on the ground. They nest in shrubbery, thickets or on the ground in fields. Song sparrows are widespread in North America and have a beautiful song that sounds like "Madge, Madge, Madge, put on your tea kettle-ettle-ettle!" Both white-crowned and white-throated sparrows are often seen in gardens and beneath feeders, busily scratching the ground in search of seeds. Most sparrows will lay four or five eggs, and they will have two and sometimes three broods each breeding season.

White-throated Sparrow

7"

Besides the sparrows on this and the previous page, there are also American tree sparrows, field sparrows, fox sparrows, swamp sparrows, grasshopper sparrows, lark sparrows, chipping sparrows and many more varieties.

White-crowned Sparrow

7"

Tundra swans flying

Bald eagle fishing

House Wren

5"

House wrens will nest in almost any small, sheltered opening, from birdhouses set out in back yards to the pockets of a jacket left outdoors. Tiny and energetic, house wrens will fiercely defend their territories. Sometimes, they will even chase away other birds that nest in the same area by tearing up their nests or puncturing their eggs. Once a male chooses a territory, he might build a base of twigs in several nest sites. When a female comes into the territory, she will choose one site, and over the twigs she will build a cup of woven grass, plants fibers, feathers and even bits of trash. House wrens eat almost nothing but insects.

Killdeer

10"

The killdeer is a shorebird that has learned to live far from water. It can be seen across North America in farm fields, at airports and on lawns as it searches for its favorite food, insects. These birds nest on open ground, often laying their eggs in gravel or short grass. If a predator approaches the nest, a killdeer may try to distract it by pretending to be injured and dragging itself away from the nest as if it has a broken wing. Once the predator is a safe distance away from the nest, the killdeer will suddenly fly off.

Tundra swans flying

Bald eagle fishing

Great egret landing

Brown pelican taking off

European Starling

8"

Both these species and those on the next two pages are exotics, birds that were not native to North America but were brought to this continent from Europe or Asia. Eight pairs of house sparrows, once know as English sparrows, were first released in New York City in 1850. A small flock of starlings was originally released in New York City in 1890. Now, both species have spread throughout North America, competing with many native species for nesting sites in tree and building cavities.

House Sparrow

6"

Mute Swan

55"

The mute swan is a European native introduced more than a century ago on the East Coast. Mute swans do not migrate and are generally silent birds, although they may hiss when approached. Ring-necked pheasants were introduced to North America from China in 1881. They are often found in brushy areas, grasslands and farm fields.

Ring-necked pheasant

33"

Tundra swans flying

Bald eagle fishing

Great egret landing

Brown pelican taking off

13"

Commonly called pigeons, rock doves may be the most familiar birds in North America. Originally European birds that nested on the ledges of sea cliffs and mountainsides, rock doves were first brought to North America in the early 1600s. They have taken so well to cities because they found similar nesting habitat on the windowsills and ledges of buildings. They construct shallow nests of grass, leaves and rubbish. They usually lay two eggs to fill their nest, but they may have as many as five broods a year. Pigeons have the ability to find their way home from great distances away using a remarkable homing instinct. Their call is a soft "Coo" or "Croo."

12"

Tundra swans flying

Bald eagle fishing

If pigeons are thought of as the doves of the cities, then mourning doves are the doves of suburban and rural areas. Mourning doves get their name from their slow moaning song "Oo-who, who, who, who." They are often seen in flocks in winter, suddenly landing beneath a bird feeder in search of fallen seeds on the ground. When trying to attract a female, a male mourning dove flies into the air, clapping its wings as it rises, and then glides to the ground in a spiral. As mourning doves take flight, their fluttering wings may create a whistling sound. Like rock doves, they may have as many as five broods each year.

79

Great egret landing

Brown pelican taking off

19"

Crows are common throughout North America despite the fact they have been intensely hunted by farmers whose crops they often feed on in great flocks, sometimes numbering tens of thousands of birds. As large as some hawks, crows have the familiar call "Caw! Caw!" Crows will eat almost anything, from corn in a field to dead animals on a highway to the nestlings of other birds. One reason why crows may be so successful is that several generations of a crow family often help to raise the young in a nest.

Common Grackle

12"

Tundra swans flying

Bald eagle fishing

Grackles can have a strange beauty. In sunlight, their feathers are rich iridescent shades of blue and purple, and their eyes are a piercing yellow. Grackles are not many people's favorite birds, though. They are large and noisy, and they may gather in flocks to take over feeders, forcing out other birds. Grackles, like crows, also have the habit of feeding on the eggs and young of other birds. In winter, they often gather in huge flocks to feed on grain and seeds.

Great egret landing

Brown pelican taking off

7"

Brown-headed cowbirds have learned an interesting way to increase the chances that their species will survive. The female cowbird lays her eggs in the nests of other birds when they are not there. Some birds, such as robins, may realize the cowbird egg isn't their own, and throw it out. But others, such as chipping sparrows, often raise the young cowbird even though it bears no resemblance to their own young and may be nearly twice the size.

Cowbird egg in chipping sparrow nest

Tundra swans flying

Bald eagle fishing

In the spring, when wild turkeys are looking for mates, the "Gobble! Gobble!" call of the male can often be heard a mile away. These large birds prefer open forests. They are weak fliers and will try to avoid predators by outrunning them. At night, turkeys will roost in trees. With the arrival of European colonists, wild turkeys gradually disappeared from much of North America, the victims of over-hunting. But today wildlife restocking programs have returned turkeys to much of their historic range.

Great egret landing

Brown pelican taking off

Canada Goose

38"

North America's most common geese, Canada geese may now be almost too common in many areas. With few predators because of their large size, and with hunting bans on them in most suburban and urban areas, Canada geese have taken up permanent residence in many lakes, reservoirs, city parks and golf courses. Their droppings can foul both the water and the land. When migrating, these geese fly in a familiar V-formation. The honking of migratory geese in fall is a sign for many people that winter is approaching.

Tundra Swan

53"

Tundra swans flying

Bald eagle fishing

Graceful and elegant in appearance, swans are the heaviest of birds that fly. Tundra swans, formerly called whistling swans, get their name from the areas in which they nest, the cold tundra regions of upper Canada and Alaska. These swans spend the winter on lakes, ponds and open marshes, sometimes assembling in great flocks numbering thousands of birds. Unlike the mute swan, the adult tundra swan has no knob on its bill, and it has a call that may sound like the trumpet of a Canada goose.

Great egret landing

Brown pelican taking off

Downy Woodpecker

6"

With their strong sharp bills, wood-peckers are able to take advantage of trees to find homes and food. They chis-el out cavities in trees to form nesting holes, and they dig beneath the bark for insects to eat. Downy woodpeckers are the smallest North American woodpeck-ers and often visit feeders. Hairy wood-peckers look very much like downy woodpeckers but are larger and shyer, generally staying in woodland areas.

Hairy Woodpecker

9"

Yellow-bellied Sapsucker

8"

Most woodpeckers use their hard bills to communicate. They drum on trees, telephone poles, metal roofs and other hard structures instead of singing the way most other birds do. Yellow-bellied sapsuckers will drill holes in trees to locate sap, their favorite food. Northern flickers are common in open woodlands and suburbs. They are often seen eating ants found on the ground.

Northern Flicker

13"

Tundra swans flying

Bald eagle fishing

Great egret landing

Brown pelican taking off

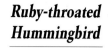
Ruby-throated Hummingbird

3½"

Hummingbirds are the world's smallest birds, but they are excellent fliers, able to dart up, down, backwards and forwards with nearly equal skill. Some hummingbirds can reach air speeds of 60 miles per hour. Hummingbirds can also hover to stay in place at a flower while they drink the sweet nectar inside with their long, straw-like bills. Despite their small size, most species migrate to Mexico and Central America for the winter.

Broad-tailed Hummingbird

4"

Rufous Hummingbird

3½"

Only one species of hummingbird nests in the East and that is the ruby-throated hummingbird. In the West, more than a dozen species can be seen during breeding season. Hummingbirds are often attracted by red flowers in gardens, and they will regularly visit feeders that contain sugar water.

Black-chinned Hummingbird

3½"

Tundra swans flying

Bald eagle fishing

Great egret landing

Brown pelican taking off

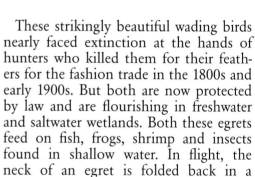

These strikingly beautiful wading birds nearly faced extinction at the hands of hunters who killed them for their feathers for the fashion trade in the 1800s and early 1900s. But both are now protected by law and are flourishing in freshwater and saltwater wetlands. Both these egrets feed on fish, frogs, shrimp and insects found in shallow water. In flight, the neck of an egret is folded back in a curve.

Snowy Egret

24"

Great Blue Heron

48"

Unlike many other long-legged wading birds, great blue herons can be found far from coastal waters. Their range extends over most of North America. This is partly because they have a more varied diet than other wading birds, and will even feed on mice and small birds. Like other herons and egrets, they spear their food with sudden jabs of their long sharp bills. Great blue herons often nest in colonies in tall trees near water, especially in trees by ponds created by beavers.

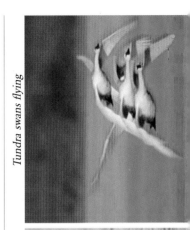

Tundra swans flying

Bald eagle fishing

Great egret landing

Brown pelican taking off

23"

Mallards are the most common ducks in North America. They will settle onto almost any lake or pond, including swimming pools! It is the female mallard who issues the familiar "Quack! Quack!" call. Mallards nest in tall grasses or reeds near water. They feed on underwater vegetation and will tip up so that their tails are in the air and their heads underwater as they search for food. A female mallard usually will lay one egg a day for 8 to 12 days. Mallards normally have only one brood of young a year.

Wood Duck

18"

Tundra swans flying

Bald eagle fishing

Wood ducks are among the most beautifully colored birds in North America. They nest in tree cavities near water and have a peculiar combination of sharpened claws and webbed feet. Wood ducks can fly at great speeds through forests, weaving their way skillfully between tree trunks and branches. Wood ducks were nearly extinct in the early 1900s because of over-hunting, but they have again become a common sight, especially in eastern North America. Wood ducks usually choose a mate in the region where they spend the winter, then the female leads the male back to the nesting grounds where she was born so that they can build their own nest.

Brown Pelican

49"

Pelicans are born to fish. With their expandable throat pouches and large bills, they skillfully scoop fish out of the water for a meal. Brown pelicans often make dramatic head-first plunges into the water to capture fish. White pelicans do not dive for fish. Instead, flocks of them may encircle an area of shallow water, beating their wings on the water and herding fish into the center to be scooped up.

White Pelican

62"

Brown Pelican in flight

Herring Gull

25"

Gulls may be thought by many to be coastal birds, but some species can also be found far inland. Both herring and ring-billed gulls are regularly seen at landfills, shopping centers and fast-food restaurants scavenging for food. Herring gulls will sometimes drop clams and other shellfish onto rocks or roadways to break the shells. Gulls often nest in large colonies on the ground.

Ring-billed Gull

19"

Tundra swans flying

Bald eagle fishing

35"

These majestic birds are among the most powerful of all birds of prey. With their sharp vision, they are able to spot fish underwater or unsuspecting waterfowl from great heights. A bald eagle will stay with its mate for life. Bald eagles typically build their huge nests in the tops of tall trees. They are primarily fish-eaters that generally nest and are seen near water, such as lakes, rivers or sea coasts. They may soar for hours high above their territories, riding on rising currents of hot air.

Peregrine Falcon

16"

Tundra swans flying

Bald eagle fishing

Peregrine falcons like to nest on the rocky ledges of cliffs and hunt over water. Increasingly, they are finding similar habitat in many cities near rivers or coasts in eastern North America. They will place their nests on skyscraper windowsills and rooftops instead of rocky ledges. A peregrine falcon will hunt pigeons and other birds for food, swooping down on the unsuspecting target in a high-speed dive.

23"

Red-tailed hawks are birds of prey, and like others of their kind they have hooked beaks and sharp talons to capture and tear apart the smaller animals they hunt. Redtails can often be seen soaring over open fields and meadows, keeping a sharp eye on the ground below for mice, snakes, frogs and other animals. However, they spend most of their time sitting in treetops beside open fields, watching for any signs of movement below.

Sharp-shinned Hawk

11"

Sharp-shinned hawks primarily hunt birds that they capture in sudden midair attacks. They sometimes attack birds at feeders. American kestrels are beautifully colored and nearly the size of robins. They are frequently seen perched on roadside telephone poles, watching the ground for mice and other small prey.

American Kestrel

9"

Tundra swans flying

Bald eagle fishing

Great Horned Owl

16"

Owls are among the most interesting birds in the world. They have large heads, short necks and large eyes that do not move in their sockets. To see in a different direction, owls have to turn their heads, and some can swivel their heads completely backwards. The great horned owl is one of the largest and most powerful of owls. With its poor sense of smell, it even includes skunks in its diet. Barn owls, with their distinctive heart-shaped faces, are often found on farms, but they also live in cities. They nest in dark holes or corners of buildings, as well as in cavities of trees or mountain cliffs.

Barn Owl

23"

Eastern Screech-Owl

9"

Owls are birds of prey that usually hunt at night. With their sensitive hearing, some owls can track their prey, such as a mouse, in the dark on the ground below just by the sound it makes as it moves. In the East, screech-owls may be either gray or reddish-brown in color. The western screech-owl has a darker bill than the eastern species and it is usually grayer.

Western Screech-Owl

9"

Tundra swans flying

Bald eagle fishing

ARCHAEOPTERYX – The first known bird; thought to have lived 140 million years ago based on fossil remains.

BIRD OF PREY – A bird that hunts other animals.

BROOD – The young of parenting birds that are hatched and cared for at the same time.

CALL – A sound a bird makes, usually briefer than a song; gives other birds information, such as a warning that danger is approaching.

EVOLUTION – The gradual process of change in birds or other living things that causes future generations to differ from their ancestors.

EXOTIC – Not native to a certain area or country; foreign.

EXTINCT – No longer existing or alive.

FORAGE – To search for food.

GLIDE – For a bird, to fly without moving its wings, allowing the flow of the air past its outstretched wings to hold it up as it gradually descends.

HABITAT – The physical conditions in which a bird or other form of wildlife normally lives.

HOVER – For a bird, to stay in one place in midair, usually by rapidly beating its wings.

LIFT – The upward force created by air as it flows around the wings of a bird, allowing the bird to fly.

MIGRATION – The seasonal movement by a bird or other animal from one area to another, usually because of a change in weather conditions or a growing scarcity of food.

MOLT – For a bird, the periodic shedding of older feathers so new feathers can be grown in their place.

NESTLING – A young bird that is still in the nest.

PERCH - To sit or rest on a branch or other support; also the place, such as a branch, where a bird sits or rests.

PLUMAGE - The feathers of a bird.

PREDATOR - An animal that captures and eats other animals.

PREEN - For a bird, to groom its plumage using its bill or claws.

RANGE - The full extent of the area in which a species of bird usually can be found. Many species have a different summer range than winter range.

ROOST - To rest or sleep; also the place where one bird or many birds rest or sleep.

SOAR - For a bird, to fly without moving its outstretched wings, allowing rising hot air to lift it higher in the sky.

SONG - A series of notes or sounds a bird makes, usually to attract a mate or to tell other birds that a certain territory is theirs.

SONGBIRD - A general name given to small perching birds, such as sparrows, finches and chickadees.

SPECIES - A group of closely related living things that can interbreed with each other. For example, snowy egrets are a species of bird.

TALON - The claw of a bird of prey or other predatory animal.

TERRITORY - An area that is defended by a bird or a pair of breeding birds against other birds so the defenders can use the area for feeding or nesting.

THERMAL - A rising flow of warm air.

Tundra swans flying

Bald eagle fishing

INDEX

A bold number indicates a page on which a photograph appears.

Barred owl

INDEX

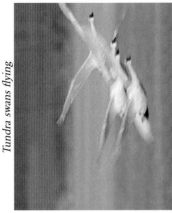

Tundra swans flying

Bald eagle fishing

American avocet

INDEX

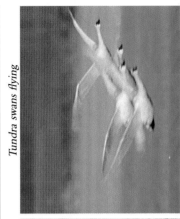

Tundra swans flying

Bald eagle fishing

Sandhill cranes dancing

PHOTO CREDITS

Tundra swans flying

Bald eagle fishing

BACKYARD BIRDS – A FAST GUIDE

American robin
Page 52

Bullock's oriole
Page 53

Baltimore oriole
Page 53

Red-winged blackbird
Page 54

Northern cardinal
Page 55

American goldfinch
Page 58

House finch
Page 59

Purple finch
Page 59

Evening grosbeak
Page 60

Blue jay
Page 65

Steller's jay
Page 65

Black-capped chickadee
Page 67

Dark-eyed junco
Page 68

White-breasted nuthatch
Page 69

Red-breasted nuthatch
Page 69

Tufted titmouse
Page 70

Plain titmouse
Page 70

Northern mockingbird
Page 71

Song sparrow
Page 72

White-crowned sparrow
Page 73

House wren
Page 74

European starling
Page 76

House sparrow
Page 76

Rock dove
Page 78

Mourning dove
Page 79

American crow
Page 80

Common grackle
Page 81

Downy woodpecker
Page 86

Ruby-throated
hummingbird
Page 88

Black-chinned
hummingbird
Page 89

Great blue herons